MAKING MINI CARDS, GIFT TAGS AND INVITATIONS

MAKING
MINI CARDS,
GIFT TAGS
AND INVITATIONS

Glennis Gilruth

GUILD OF MASTER CRAFTSMAN PUBLICATIONS LTD

First published 2000 by
Guild of Master Craftsman Publications Ltd
166 High Street, Lewes
East Sussex, BN7 1XU

Photographs by Stephen Hepworth
Text and illustrations © Glennis Gilruth 2000
© in the Work GMC Publications Ltd

Reprinted 2001, 2002, 2003, 2004

ISBN 1 86108 170 7

British Library Cataloguing in Publication Data
A catalogue record of this book is available from the British Library

Cover design by Ian Smith, GMC Design Studio
Book design by Jane Hawkins
Typefaces: Amerigo and Frutiger

Colour orgination by Viscan Graphics P.L (Singapore)
Printed and bound by Kyodo Printing (Singapore)

CONTENTS

INTRODUCTION

If you enjoy colour, texture, beautiful papers, threads, beads, ink and paint, then you will love creating mini cards. Mini cards are fun to make and, from the delighted response I have encountered, they are a pleasure to receive. Small is beautiful and, whether simple or sophisticated, mini cards are ideal as gift tags, invitations, greetings cards, thank you notes, or just to say 'hello'. The designs in this book use simple shapes, eye-catching papers in beautiful colours and a multitude of small accessories. I hope that you, like me, will find as much pleasure in decorating paper, finding exciting handmade papers and tracking down small adornments, as you do in creating your mini cards.

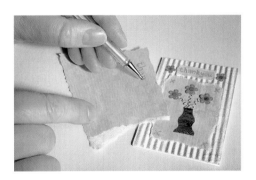

Glennis Gilruth

1

BASIC EQUIPMENT & MATERIALS

The ever-widening range of craft equipment and art materials available in shops and by mail order is good news, because you can now use decorative scissors and punches, perforate, crimp and incorporate fabulous handmade papers, paper yarns, craft ribbons, beads and paint finishes into your designs.

Yarns, threads and beads

When making mini cards, a little goes a long way and you can start with just a few pieces of equipment and materials, adding more as you progress. If you enjoy art and craft, you may already have many useful items to hand and will certainly know your way around an art store. However, if you are new to art and craft, I hope that the following pages will remove the mystery but still retain the magic!

Your basic equipment and materials should include:
- Marking out and cutting equipment
- Colouring materials
- Adhesives
- Paper and card
- Ribbon, yarn, beads

MARKING OUT AND CUTTING EQUIPMENT
Most of the cutting in the following projects can be done with scissors; however, when trimming straight edges, a craft knife or scalpel is better and a self-healing cutting mat is essential. Cutting mats are formed from a sandwich of plastics which protect your work surface and help to prevent your blade from becoming blunt. The surface grid is extremely useful when measuring and cutting right angles. Never use a wooden board as a cutting surface because, not only will the wood grip your blade, making it difficult to control the cut, but it will also blunt a blade quite rapidly.

MARKING OUT AND CUTTING EQUIPMENT

- Propelling pencil (more accurate than ordinary pencil)
- Soft eraser
- Plastic ruler for measuring and marking out (do not use for cutting against)
- Metal safety ruler for cutting against
- Knitting needle or medium-point embossing stylus (for scoring card)
- Scissors – plain and decorative – as many pairs as you can get!
- Craft knife (or scalpel) and spare blades
- Self-healing cutting mat

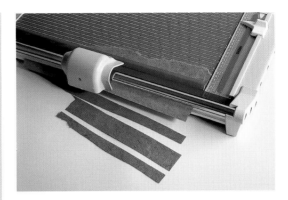

A rotary cutter is a worthwhile investment

COLOURING MATERIALS

- Paintbrushes
- Inks and paints
- Crayons
- Felt-tip pens
- Gel pens

Paintbrushes To make the mini cards illustrated you need only a medium-size flat brush for colouring paper, a fine round brush for detail, and some old brushes and sponge for paint effects.

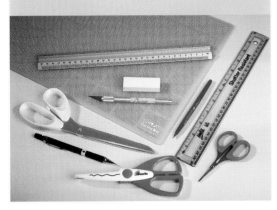

A selection of marking out and cutting equipment

Serious equipment! I use a rotary cutter for trimming paper and card. These can be quite expensive, but they do protect fingers and are great for accurate cutting of straight edges. A rotary cutter will ensure perfect right angles, allow you to trim the tiniest sliver from paper and card, and is invaluable when card-making or pursuing any papercraft activity.

A wide variety of colouring materials can be used

Inks and paints Inks and paints are ideal for colouring paper and are available in water-based or acrylic format in a wide array of colours, plus pearlised and metallic effects. Ink can be used full strength for a vibrant, bold effect or diluted to provide a pale, subtle wash with a lovely translucent quality. Liquid acrylic paint can be used full strength for an opaque look, thinned slightly for an intense wash or watered down for a semi-transparent effect.

Experimentation is the key when working with inks and paints – try different papers, brushes, brushstrokes, colour/media mixes and strengths.

Crayons Subtle colour effects can be created with coloured pencils. Try to use good quality crayons which impart rich colour without too much pressure.

Good quality crayons will impart rich colour to your design

Pens A selection of coloured pens is useful when applying pattern to inked or painted paper, or writing greetings or messages. I particularly like gel ink pens which are obtainable in a range of opaque candy colours, brights and metallics in different nib shapes.

Gel ink pens are very effective on coloured paper

ADHESIVES
The type of glue you need will depend on the job you are doing. For the projects in this book I have used:
- PVA (polyvinyl acetate), a multipurpose white liquid adhesive which dries clear, and is sold under many brand names.
- Glue stick, e.g. Pritt Stick
- Spray adhesive

 Safety Hint: it is essential to observe the instructions on adhesives, especially sprays. When using spray adhesive I place the item to be sprayed on a large cardboard tray, which I keep especially for that purpose, and I do all spraying outdoors.

PAPER AND CARD

Paper and card are essential basic materials and you will find a huge selection in art and craft shops, also from specialist paper suppliers who advertise in art and craft magazines. If you are keen to recycle or keep costs down, don't forget to have a look at used giftwrap or food and cosmetic packaging before you discard them, as they often contain attractive foil or interesting areas of colour, retrievable card, or yarn.

Food packaging often contains foiled card

Many of the projects in this book have a base of brilliant white, smooth watercolour paper. I used Frisk 320gsm which is thick enough to take glue and paint with minimal distortion, yet smooth and soft enough to cut and fold cleanly.

RIBBON, YARN AND BEADS ETC.

Ribbon, cord or yarn can add exciting texture or colour to your mini cards and, as most are inexpensive, it's easy to gather quite a collection. A small piece of ribbon may be just the thing you need for a particular design, so don't discard any scraps. When buying beads, have a look at jewellery findings for other interesting items such as tiny pieces of chain or metal motifs. Look out for attractive sequins and threads, as these can all add colour and texture to your designs, or you can create small motifs in synthetic modelling clay.

CHAPTER TWO

SAFETY MEASURES

As in all craft activities, safety precautions should be observed.

 Pay attention to the safety hints throughout the book. Look out for this balloon.

KNIVES AND SCISSORS

Sharp knives and scissors are easier to use than blunt ones but accidents can happen so, when cutting, bear these rules in mind:

- Find a firm and tidy work surface.
- Never cut directly towards yourself.
- If cutting against a ruler, always use a metal safety ruler which protects your fingers.
- When not in use, retract knife blades or replace blade covers.
- Keep all sharp implements, such as scissors, needles and knives, away from the edge of your work surface and preferably in a tray or box.
- Dispose of used blades carefully.

ADHESIVES AND PAINT

Make sure you have read and understood the manufacturer's recommendations regarding use and storage before you start working with adhesives and paints.

GENERAL

When creating your cards, ensure that all parts of the design are firmly attached, especially beads. Apart from the disappointment of your design falling apart, there is a danger that children and pets will swallow pieces. **Never give cards with attached pieces of decoration or beads to very small children.**

CHAPTER THREE

DECORATIVE TECHNIQUES

Whether a mini greetings card, a gift tag or an invitation, most of the designs in this book comprise a background and a motif, and by adding an envelope, string or different base, you can transform any design to suit your purposes.

GETTING STARTED

Beautiful materials, a special person or occasion are all inspirational and will help you to choose a theme. Simply gathering together papers, ribbons, cords and beads will suggest colour schemes and motifs. Every project in this book has an element of collage – shapes and materials brought together. For me, the attraction of collage is the freedom to use practically any material I wish and the thrill of placing colours and textures which complement and contrast, even in the small scale of these designs.

DECORATING PAPER

Although paper can be found in a myriad of colours and patterns it is extremely enjoyable to colour or decorate your own for use as a background or for collage on your mini card designs – it can also be used for making envelopes, or even as gift wrap.

Most of these card projects require just a small amount of coloured or decorated paper, and you can prepare small pieces and flatten them inside an old telephone directory. However, if you are decorating larger sheets of paper, anything over A4, I would advise stretching and drying it before you apply 'wet' colour, such as ink or paint (see pages 8-9).

Painted paper for collage use will cut and tear more effectively if you thin the paint (whether acrylic or water based) and apply it as a wash. Strong colour will still be achieved but, rather than sitting on top of the paper, it will be absorbed into the paper, making cutting and tearing easier.

Practical Hint: when decorating paper for gift wrapping, select a medium to lightweight paper which will be easier to handle and fold when wrapping around a parcel.

Stretching and colouring paper When painting paper, you may have noticed that it tends to buckle and may remain distorted, even after drying, because the fibres in the paper stretch and shrink at different rates. By stretching your paper before you apply 'wet' colour such as ink or paint, you can control this distortion and produce beautifully flat, coloured or decorated paper.

When stretching paper, the trick is to have everything to hand before you start. You may have some initial hiccups with creases, bubbles or tears, but you will soon become expert and develop your own technique.

EQUIPMENT

- Board, smooth plywood or similar, which is larger than your piece of paper
- Brown-paper gumstrip
- Sponge
- Clean water
- Colouring materials, e.g. paint or ink
- Brush for applying colouring materials

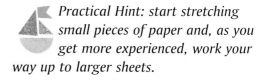 *Practical Hint: start stretching small pieces of paper and, as you get more experienced, work your way up to larger sheets.*

STEP 1 Cut four strips of brown-paper gumstrip – one for each edge of the paper – and keep them to hand, but dry.

STEP 2 Lay the paper centrally on the stretching board, reverse side up. Damp the paper with a wet sponge. Then, quickly lift the paper, turn it over, again placing it in the middle of the board, and damp the other side. Avoid rubbing the paper as this will damage the surface. (You will find that lightweight paper needs damping on one side only. It will buckle immediately, but don't panic, you will still achieve a smooth result.)

STEP 3 Damp the brown-paper gumstrip with your sponge and quickly tape the paper to the board, ignoring any ripples or small creases. When the tape is in place you can gently dab up any obvious puddles with your sponge, taking care not to rub the paper.

STEP 4 Place the board on a flat surface to dry for about an hour. When you return you will be amazed at the smooth, drum-like surface of the stretched paper, which you can now colour or decorate while still attached to the board. Ripples may appear while you are working on your paper, but these will disappear again on drying.

STEP 5 After colouring or decorating your paper, allow it to dry completely before you slit through the brown-paper gumstrip and remove the paper from the board.

Practical Hint: to clean your board, damp any remaining gumstrip thoroughly then leave for a few minutes and it will lift off quite easily without the need for scraping. Wipe the board down, to remove remaining traces of gum.

PAINT EFFECTS

As well as simply applying colour to paper, you can add decorative finishes such as splatter, crackle, scumble, dry brush, printing and stencilling.

Splatter Ink or paint splatter is great fun to do, even if the results are unpredictable! It can be a messy process, so washable, water-based pigments are preferable to waterproof inks.

Ink can be difficult as, being a thin liquid, it tends to splash and drip. Paint is easier, but won't work if it's too thick, so a few experiments are required. The only equipment needed is an old toothbrush or short-haired bristle paintbrush, plus a lollipop stick or something similar.

Splattering is simple: lightly load your brush with ink or paint and draw a lollipop stick across the bristles, so that a spray of ink or paint leaves the brush. Always point the brush away from you and draw the stick towards you or you will get a splattered face!

 *Practical Hint: a large cardboard box makes an effective shield. Either put the paper in the box while splattering onto it, or cut the box up and use the pieces as a protective shield.*

Splattering – note the correct technique!

Your results will depend on the consistency of the ink or paint, the size and shape of the brush, and the distance you are working from the paper. Don't be afraid to experiment until you find the effect you want.

Style Hint: why not try splattering the same piece of paper with two or three different colours? For even more variation, splatter wet on wet.

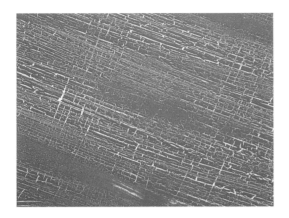

Crackle finish

Crackle finish Crackleglaze is extremely attractive and there are now products specifically for smaller scale crafts which can be used to obtain a crackle finish on paper. Even the most subtle crackled effect on a small part of a design can make a difference.

Scumble can be used to add colour to motifs

Scumble has the appearance of a softly broken blending of one colour over another. The easiest way to achieve this effect is to use an old brush with separated and splayed bristles, or you can use a small piece of sponge (a piece torn from a cheap, synthetic sponge is ideal). Coat the brush or sponge very lightly with paint then, on a wad of kitchen roll, wipe off as much as you can. Apply the paint in a gentle, dabbing motion. The result should be smudgy and delicate, rather as if you are running out of paint.

Flat brush painting brings spontaneity to painted shapes

Flat brush painting To achieve attractive, painterly areas of colour, take a short-haired, flat bristle brush and apply paint in swift, deliberate strokes. (Don't try to 'tidy up' the edges.)

Printing Simple shapes cut from an eraser can be used to print decorations on your cards, papers or envelopes, using an ink pad or paint.

Practical Hint: acrylic paint tends to dry fairly quickly so dispense it in small amounts onto a wad of kitchen roll and use this as a printing pad: wipe off the paint until there is just enough – the least paint gives the best effect when printing or stencilling.

Simple shapes can be cut from an eraser

Stencilling is a quick and effective method of decoration. A simple stencil cut from card will generally last long enough for a small project. Apply paint sparingly with a soft stencil brush or sponge in a gentle, dabbing motion, as when scumbling. Alternatively, you could use soft crayon.

Style Hint: intricate stencils, like this paw print, can be cut from a piece of paper with a decorative punch – if the paper stencil gets a bit soggy you can quickly make another.

Use less paint for the best effect

Practical Hints:
● Try cutting a tiny stencil from the sticky part of a post-it note and it will stay in place without damaging the paper.
● Wipe the stencil brush on a wad of kitchen roll until there is a minimum of paint on the brush.
● Work inwards from the edges of the stencil.
● Ensure the back of the stencil is clean before repositioning.

FOLDING PAPER AND CARD

As when tearing paper and card, the grain (the way the fibres lie) may make it easier to fold in one direction than the other, i.e. it is easier to fold and tear with the grain than against it. For these small-scale projects, however, this should not cause any difficulty.

Clean, crisp folds are the basis of many designs and are very easy to achieve:

STEP 1 Using a propelling pencil and ruler, lightly mark the centre point of your paper or card, top and bottom.

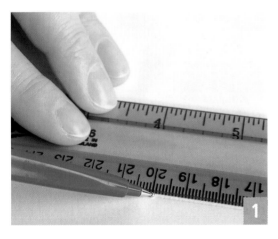

STEP 2 Score lightly between the marks with an embossing stylus or knitting needle.

STEP 3 Fold over gently, but don't rub down the crease with your fingers or you may transfer natural oils from your hands to the card.

STEP 4 Place a clean piece of paper over the crease and rub it with the back of a spoon to make a clean, crisp fold.

Practical Hint: when folding crepe paper or soft paper, take extra care to score the crease very lightly so that the paper does not stretch and make a 'wavy' fold.

INSERTS

Flat or folded leaves of paper with a message can be added inside mini designs. These can be straight edged, torn, perforated or cut with decorative scissors, according to your design, then held in place with a light touch of glue or decorative stitching.

Multi-coloured stamp pads can add extra fun

Insert held in place with decorative stitching

ADDING YOUR MESSAGE

Greetings can be added to many of these designs and a handwritten message looks charming on a handmade card. If you are unsure about adding lettering to your card, try placing it on a small motif and then incorporate it into your design. Gel pens with opaque coloured inks are ideal for writing on coloured paper. Text can also be produced on a word processor or with a rubber stamp. If you want to write or stamp directly onto your design it is a good idea to determine how much space your message will need and whether the paper is suitable.

Rubber stamps are particularly useful for party invitations as you just need to complete the details by hand.

For those occasions when you plan to make a large number of cards, you could consider a custom-made stamp, as used on this change-of-address card.

Style Hint: 'loosen up' and practise writing or stamping your message before working directly on your design.

Practical Hint: if your design has an element of 3D, such as beads or crimped paper, complete all stamping while still at the 'flat' stage or it will be difficult to apply the stamp.

GLUING

PVA or glue stick can be used for most parts of your mini cards. When using PVA take care not to use too much because, as a 'wet' adhesive, it can distort paper or card. If you find that glue has warped your work, allow it to dry fully then try pressing it flat under a heavy book for a while.

Practical Hint: PVA tends to clog ordinary paintbrushes so I use a silicone wedge brush. Any glue which happens to dry on it peels off quite easily.

A wedge brush is easy to clean

Spray adhesive is ideal for bonding lightweight papers and craft ribbon to paper and card because it glues without over-wetting. For safety hints on using spray adhesive, please see the Adhesives section (page 4).

Gluing small pieces PVA is the best glue to use when attaching a small piece, such as a tiny flower, to your design. Using a cocktail stick, apply a dab to the background rather than the flower itself. It will then be much easier to place the small piece accurately.

Apply glue to the background

Gluing pompoms You will need plenty of adhesive when attaching fluffy materials such as pompoms, because the fibres tend to absorb the glue. PVA is the most effective, but take care not to over-wet the background you are attaching to, and remember that the more adhesive you use the longer it will take to dry, so try to leave it undisturbed for a while.

EMBOSSED EFFECT

You can achieve an embossed effect on thick, soft watercolour paper by drawing into the paper with a stylus or by cutting shapes in the same thick paper and gluing them in place. Watercolour paper such as Frisk 320gsm is ideal for this type of work because though thick, it is soft, smooth and easy to cut (see Cutting Motifs, below right, for more information). Colour can be added with crayon or rub-down foil, as shown in these designs.

Here, colour highlights the embossed effects

MOTIFS

Cut motifs in a continuous direction

Cutting motifs To obtain a smooth, cushioned edge when cutting watercolour paper motifs, use small, sharp, narrow scissors and, if right-handed, cut the motif in a continuous anticlockwise direction. The action of the scissor blades on thick, soft paper seems to press it slightly before cutting it, thus making a smooth edge. To create this same smooth effect, a left-handed person should use left-handed scissors in a continuous clockwise direction.

Foil covered motifs A sleek, embossed foil-look can be achieved by cutting a shape from watercolour paper, then covering it with foiled paper (i.e. paper with a foiled surface, not ordinary silver paper or aluminium foil).

YOU WILL NEED:

- A motif cut from thick, smooth, water-colour paper (I use this type of paper rather than card for this effect because paper is softer and, when the shape is cut out, the edges have a cushioned effect, rather than a hard angled cut)

- A piece of foiled paper, slightly bigger than the motif

STEP 1 Take the motif and apply glue stick to one flat side and all around the thickness of it, then place it, glue side down, on the reverse of the foiled paper.

STEP 2 Turn the foiled paper over and rub it lightly so that you can see the underlying motif, then run a medium-point stylus around the edge of the motif, so that the foiled paper is moulded over the shape, giving a sculpted effect.

STEP 3 Allow the glue to dry then, using small, sharp scissors, trim away the excess foil.

Style Hint: to give your motif an attractive matt sheen, use a medium-point stylus to scribble on the reverse of the foiled paper before you apply it to your motif.

Paper-covered shapes An interesting effect can be created by loosely covering a simple shape, such as a heart or a square, in soft paper. A wrap-around edge, secured at the back, leaves the paper loose on the front of the motif giving a cushioned appearance.

The base shape should be cut from firm card, but the covering paper needs to be pliable so that you can mould it, rather like fabric, around the shape.

YOU WILL NEED:

- A shape cut from firm card.
- A similar shape (about 5mm larger all around) in soft, pliable paper (soft handmade papers are good for this).
- Small, sharp scissors
- Glue stick

STEP 1 Centre the card shape on the paper shape and snip the paper shape at corners and around curves, leaving an intact 1mm ($\frac{1}{32}$in) margin around the card shape.

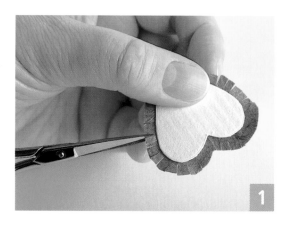

STEP 2 Wrap the snipped edge around the back of the card shape, moulding smoothly around any curves, then glue it down.

OTHER TEXTURE EFFECTS

Sewing paper When sewing paper, it is easier and more controllable to first make pilot holes using a paper piercer and an old mouse mat, as shown here, then use a darning needle to enlarge the holes to the required size.

Making holes with a paper piercer

 Safety Hint: don't put your fingers around the back of card or paper when you are making holes with a paper piercer or needle.

Paper yarn and natural or synthetic raffia are ideal when sewing paper because you can thread these through holes without using a needle. When using needle and thread, press the paper back into place around the stitch holes for a neater finish.

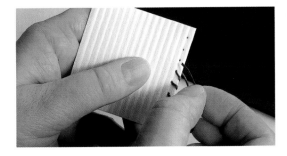

Paper yarn threads very easily

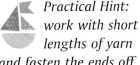 *Practical Hint: work with short lengths of yarn and fasten the ends off with a tiny strip of masking tape at the back of your work.*

Laminating paper If you find an attractive paper which is too lightweight or soft for your purposes, it can be laminated, or bonded, to backing paper. Spray adhesive or glue stick gives the best results. Choose the colour of the backing paper carefully. A white backing paper will lighten or brighten the surface colour, whereas a toning backing paper usually deepens the colour.

Pen 'stitching' Simulated stitches can be drawn with a gel ink pen. To make a stitch, press the point of the pen into the paper to make a dot then, without lifting the pen from the paper, draw a short line for the stitch and finish with another impressed dot.

Pen stitching is a quick alternative

DECORATIVE TIES

Knots and stitches Decorative knots and running stitches, whilst giving the appearance of attaching pieces of paper, don't actually need to be sewn through more than one layer. Just make knots or stitches through the top layer of paper, fasten the ends of the thread with a tiny strip of masking tape at the back of the paper, then glue the stitched paper in position.

Bows When adding a bow make sure that the material, as well as the colour, co-ordinates with your design.

Style Hint: a bow will look more attractive if you don't pull the knot too tight. Instead, secure the loops in position with a dab of PVA.

Plaiting or braiding Plaited or braided threads can be used to make loops and decorative bows. Try mixing the materials you use such as flat and round yarns or, as shown here, paper yarns, narrow silk ribbons and stranded embroidery threads.

Try mixing materials when plaiting or braiding

Cords Attractive cords made from yarn, raffia or even thin ribbon can dress up your designs. A basic twisted cord can be made as follows:

STEP 1 Take a length of yarn and use sticky tape to fasten one end to your work surface.

STEP 2 Tape the other end of the yarn to a pencil.

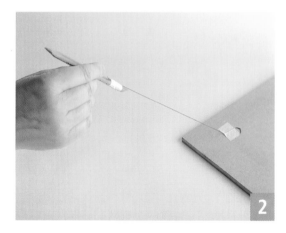

STEP 3 Roll the pencil continuously in one direction, twisting the cord. When the yarn has enough tension it will try to twist together.

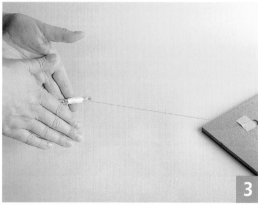

STEP 4 Keeping the yarn taut, pinch it together at the halfway point, then allow the twist to form, adding more twist if required.

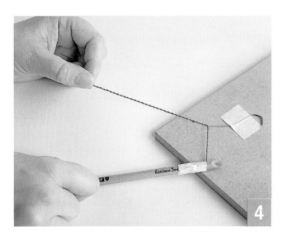

STEP 5 Keeping both ends of the yarn firmly nipped together, cut them free from the sticky tape and make a knot to hold the twist.

The materials you use and the tension of the twist will determine the finished length of your cord. Try twisting different colours and materials together.

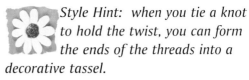

Style Hint: when you tie a knot to hold the twist, you can form the ends of the threads into a decorative tassel.

Spirals A decorative spiral can be made by winding a short length of paper-covered wire around a pencil, then flattening it out.

TEARING PAPER

If you want to tear a particular shape, you will find it much easier if you cut the shape from scrap paper and use this as a template to tear around. Printed or painted paper shows the original colour of the paper when it is torn and this can be used to decorative effect.

 Style Hint: look at the difference between a left hand and right hand tear.

COLLAGE

Arrange all collage pieces satisfactorily before you glue any into place. When gluing small pieces, such as this little boat, it is easier to apply a small dab of glue to the background, with a cocktail stick.

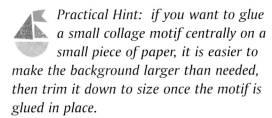 *Practical Hint: if you want to glue a small collage motif centrally on a small piece of paper, it is easier to make the background larger than needed, then trim it down to size once the motif is glued in place.*

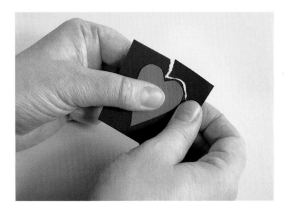

Tearing around a template

Paper with a subtle crackled effect adds extra detail to this collage boat

DECORATIVE PAPER PUNCHES

Examples of decorative paper punches

Decorative paper punches, available as single motifs, rows of motifs, or corner designs, are great time savers, especially if you are making cards in multiples. A bonus is that you can use the punched motif or the punched hole (or both) as part of your design. Motifs can be applied simply as decoration but these flower shapes can actually be made into small flowers. (See Making Flowers, Wiggly Stem Flower, page 28).

Tiny flowers made with decorative paper punch

Practical Hint: best results are obtained with light- to medium-weight papers – press the punch with a firm movement, but don't be heavy-handed. Photocopy paper can be used to support delicate papers or tissue whilst punching out shapes.

DECORATIVE SCISSORS

Decorative scissors are great for adding a fancy edge to card and paper but they can also be used to create pattern, as here on this hot air balloon, where a few different scissors were used to cut narrow strips of brightly inked paper. The strips were then glued onto white card and the balloon shape was cut out. You can also use this technique to make patterns for motifs such as hearts, fishes or Easter eggs.

Patterns can be made with decorative scissors

Practical Hint: when making a long cut, make sure you maintain continuity by matching up with the preceding pattern each time you reposition the scissors.

PUNCH WHEEL

Attractive perforated and torn edges can be made with a small gadget called a punch wheel. This can also be used to decorate paper, as shown here, where I have first applied a simple stamped pattern then emphasised this with perforated lines to produce a tiny quilted effect.

The punch wheel can enhance pattern

PAPER CRIMPER

Crimped paper isn't always available in the exact colour you need, so a paper crimper is invaluable. For extra variation you can crimp decorated paper, foil, stiffened fabric or ribbon. You can even crimp wire and paper-covered wire.

Crimped paper adds an extra dimension

GLITTERGLAZE

Glitterglaze is exactly as it sounds: iridescent particles carried in a clear glaze which dries to a smooth, sparkly finish. It can be applied as a glaze over acrylic paint or directly to coloured paper.

SYNTHETIC MODELLING CLAY

Modelling clay and cutters

Synthetic modelling clay, such as Fimo, Formello or Sculpey, makes excellent motifs. It is pliable, can be hardened in a domestic oven and is available in a large range of colours, but you can use any colour and paint it, as I have done with the motifs shown here.

 Safety Hint: apply paint only after the hardening and cooling process. Once painted, motifs cannot again be heated in an oven.

Mini cards and tags call for small motifs and a great starting point is to use tiny sugarcraft cutters to make basic shapes.

STEP 1 Take a small piece of clay and knead to soften, then place on a piece of baking foil and flatten it out to about 3mm (⅛in) thick. Remember, don't make your motif too heavy or thick.

STEP 2 Use a sugarcraft cutter to cut out the basic shape then, leaving the motif in place on the foil, remove the excess clay around it.

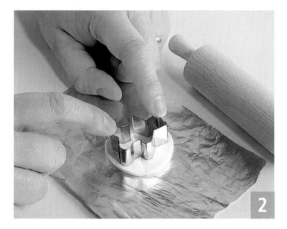

STEP 3 At this point you can keep the basic shape, add details or adjust the shape, as required. Following the instructions on the packaging, harden the clay in the oven then allow it to cool.

Practical Hint: don't try to lift these small motifs from the foil until after they have been hardened and cooled, or you may disturb the shape.

STEP 4 After cooling, apply a couple of coats of white acrylic gesso, which makes an ideal undercoat (and is also useful for introducing surface texture if required). Decorations or details can then be added in acrylic paint or watercolour.

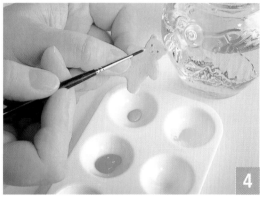

Style Hint: as shown with this teddy bear motif, which started as a basic shape, you can add texture by pressing the soft clay with fabric, or use modelling tools to add extra shape and detail.

Impress materials in the soft clay to add texture

CRAFT RIBBON
Stiffened cotton craft ribbon resists fraying and is ideal for cutting into decorative shapes.

Craft ribbon resists fraying

METAL LEAF AND RUB-DOWN FOIL
Metal leaf and rub-down foil are available in copper, silver, shades of gold and metallic colours. The basic method is to apply size or special adhesive to the area to be foiled, using a small brush for detailed areas. The adhesive is exceptionally tacky and does tend to spoil brushes unless washed immediately after use, so don't use your best paintbrush. For small applications, try using a cocktail stick.

Applying the metal leaf or foil

When the adhesive is tacky-dry, the metal leaf or foil is smoothed on. Refer to packaging for individual brand instructions. Any residual tackiness after application of the foil can be remedied with a light trace of talcum powder.

 Style Hint: add extra excitement to metal finishes by teaming matt gold with bright gold, or silver with copper etc.

3D PAINT
3D paints are fun to use and certainly do add an extra dimension. They are available in gloss, pearl and sparkly finishes and are applied directly from the bottle, via a nozzle, rather like icing a cake. Have a quick practice but don't try to make your drawings too perfect because everyone has their own individual style, as in handwriting, be it neat or quirky.

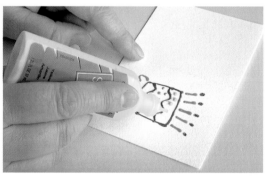

3D paint applied through a nozzle

 Practical Hint: these paints are very thick so allow plenty of drying time.

THIN METAL SHEET

Thin metal sheet is available in gold, silver or copper colour. It is quite easy to work with and you can cut it with ordinary scissors, but it can be extremely sharp and requires careful handling; I suggest, therefore, that any motifs you cut should have no sharp angles and that you take great care when disposing of trimmings. In experiments I found that an embossed line around the edge of a motif made it easier to cut out and better to handle.

To make a motif such as this fish you will need an old magazine or mouse mat to rest on, a medium-point embossing stylus and a small pair of scissors (don't use your best ones!).

STEP 1 Cut a piece from the metal sheet, big enough for your motif plus a couple of centimetres (¾in) around it.

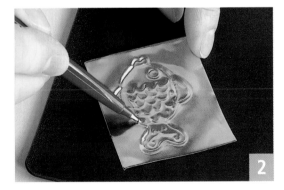

STEP 2 Rest the piece of metal sheet on a magazine or mouse mat, and draw and decorate your motif using enough pressure to impress the design into the metal.

Note that this is the reverse side of the motif, so if you are making, for example, a fish, it will eventually face the other way.

STEP 3 Turn the metal sheet over. The drawing you have done with the stylus will have an embossed appearance on this side of the metal sheet.

STEP 4 Carefully cut out your motif with small scissors, avoiding leaving sharp burrs along the way, and carefully disposing of any small trimmings.

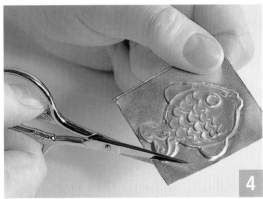

STEP 5 Use a good quality PVA to attach the motif to your design.

 Safety Hint: remember that this metal sheet can be very sharp and should be kept away from small children. Always check motifs for sharp edges before gluing them firmly in place.

MAKING FLOWERS

Wiggly stem flower

Flower head
- Using the decorative flower-shaped punch, cut out a flower shape.
- Using small scissors, cut a tiny circle of foiled paper for the flower centre.
- Using PVA, attach flower centre. (Do this now so that you have a flat surface to press against; leave any pen or paint decorations until later.)

Flower stem
Pass a length of fine craft wire through the paper crimper and cut a piece for your flower stem.

Assemble and finish
- Place the flower face down and, using a small blob of PVA adhesive, carefully glue the stem to the back of the flower and leave to dry.
- When the adhesive is dry, add any pen or paint decorations.

 Style Hint: try using 3D paint or a small glass bead for the flower centre

Never give cards with attached pieces of decoration or beads to very small children.

EQUIPMENT:

To make this flower you will need basic tools, plus:
- Paper crimper
- Flower-shaped punch

MATERIALS:

- Scraps of paper – anything from hand-made paper to painted paper but nothing too thick or strong
- Scrap of foiled paper
- Fine craft wire – I have used a wire wound with fine green thread but you could also use coloured wire or fine paper-covered wire
- PVA adhesive

Straight stem flower

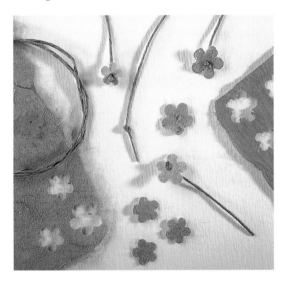

EQUIPMENT:

To make this flower you will need basic tools, plus:
- Flower-shaped punch
- Needle (slightly thicker than the paper yarn)

MATERIALS:

- Scraps of paper – anything from hand-made paper to painted paper but nothing too thick or strong
- Paper yarn

Flower head
- Using the decorative flower shaped punch, cut out a flower shape.
- Pass the needle through the centre of the flower.

Flower stem
- Take a length of paper yarn and tie a knot at the end. (Don't worry about making the knot right at the end; you can trim, close to the knot, later.)
- Cut the yarn approx. 30mm (1¼in) from the knot to form a flower stem.

Assembly
- Thread the stem through the hole in the flower so that the flower rests under the knot. If it tends to slip down the stem, add a small dab of PVA under the flower to hold it firmly in place.
- Trim the yarn down to the knot.

 Style Hint: try threading two punched flower shapes, a smaller one on top of a larger one, on one stem, possibly in two toning colours.

Crimped flower

EQUIPMENT:

To make this flower you will need basic tools, plus:
- Paper crimper

MATERIALS:

- Scraps of paper – anything which will hold crimps
- Seed beads

Method
- Crimp the paper.
- Make a template of the petal shape and, taking care not to flatten the crimps, cut out five petals with the crimps following the same direction.
- Cut a small circle of scrap card about 10mm (½in) diameter (as a base) and place a blob of PVA adhesive in the centre.
- Arrange the petals so that the centre points rest in the adhesive and leave to dry.
- Place a small blob of PVA adhesive in the centre of the flower and add glass beads then leave to dry.

 Style Hint: the bead centre covers the joining of the petals and adds an extra dimension.

Curved petal flower with crimped stem

EQUIPMENT:

To make a curved petal flower you will need basic tools, plus:
- Paper crimper
- Blunt scissors

MATERIALS:

- Scraps of paper (nothing too soft or textured or it will not curve successfully)
- Paper-covered wire

Flower head
- Cut a circle of paper, diameter approximately 45mm (1¾in), and work around the edge making snips to form the petals.
- Using a blunt pair of scissors, curl each petal by pulling it between your thumb and the blade.

Flower stem and spiral in centre of flower
- Run a short length of paper-covered wire through the paper crimper.
- Make a spiral for the centre of the flower by wrapping the crimped wire around a pencil and trimming off the excess.
- Cut a length of the crimped wire for the flower stem.
- Unwind a piece of paper from the paper-covered wire and cut two leaf shapes.

Assembly

Using PVA adhesive, glue the spiral in the centre front of the flower and the stem to the back of the flower, then glue the leaves to the stem.

 Style Hint: you can curve the petals under or over.

Paper and collage flower

EQUIPMENT:
To make this flower in a pot you will need basic tools, plus:
● Medium-point embossing stylus
MATERIALS:
● Scraps of gold foiled paper
● Scraps of fabric
● Glue stick

Method

- Use the embossing stylus to make a random pattern on the reverse of the gold foiled paper. This will show on the front as an attractive matt effect.
- Cut out the shapes for the flower, leaves, and pot.

- When you have prepared a background for your collage design, arrange as shown and glue down carefully, using glue stick.
- When the glue is dry you can use the embossing stylus to add further details to gold areas, such as veins on the leaves.

 Style Hint: when making a little motif like this flower in a pot, don't be too exact when cutting and arranging your shapes – apply your personal touch.

Paper punch flower:
The petals of this flower are made with heart and flower-shaped paper punches and the centre is a touch of 3D bead paint.

Method
- Using the decorative paper punches, make five hearts and a flower.
- When you have prepared a background, first glue the small punched flower in position.
- Glue the heart shapes around the flower, as shown.
- Add a bead of 3D paint and leave to dry.

 Style Hint: try switching around, putting the heart in the centre and flowers round the edge.

EQUIPMENT:

To make this flower you will need basic tools, plus:
- Heart-shaped paper punch
- Flower-shaped paper punch

MATERIALS:

- Scraps of paper – anything from handmade paper to painted paper but nothing too thick or strong
- 3D bead paint
- Glue stick (if using lightweight paper)
- PVA adhesive (if using medium-weight paper for punched shapes)

FINISHING TOUCHES

Every project in this book can be adapted to make a mini card, a gift tag, or an invitation, and a tie or decorative envelope can be added to any design.

Shaped designs such as the Hearts, Happy Dog and Cosy Cat could be attached to a folded base to transform them into mini greetings cards, and a message motif can be added to many designs.

Folded designs can be made as single panels and used as flat gift tags.

Beautiful presentation enhances a gift

Practical Hint: keep any small scraps of paper, beads etc. as these can be used to add the finishing touches to a string or decorative envelope.

Gift tags Gift tags can be tucked under the string on a parcel, put in a small envelope, or attached with a tie. When adding an envelope or string to a gift tag, try to co-ordinate the colour and material with the tag and gift wrap.

Strings and loops can be decorated with beads or tiny motifs. If using beads, do ensure that they are knotted firmly in place. Here are a few different ways to attach a string:

Different ways to add strings and loops

- Loop string over the fold of the card.
- Thread string through hole.
- Attach a loop of string with glue or knots, like a 'handle'.
- Stitch the string along the fold.

DECORATIVE ENVELOPES

rectangle with a triangular flap on each side and, when folded in place, the flaps overlap slightly so that the card is completely enclosed.

USEFUL EQUIPMENT WHEN MAKING ENVELOPES

- Self-healing cutting mat with surface grid
- Plastic measuring ruler
- Propelling pencil (more accurate than pencil)
- Medium-point stylus or knitting needle (for scoring folds)
- Scissors or craft knife and safety ruler
- Scrap paper

As the perfect complement to your work, what could be nicer than a co-ordinating decorative envelope? You can make your own envelope, or customise a ready-made with stencilling or a decorative seal which echoes elements of your design in colour, materials or motif. When attaching a seal, the lightest touch of glue ensures that it will open without tearing. (Small or decorative envelopes will need the added protection of a regular envelope when sent by mail.)

Making envelopes When making an envelope, always make a template in scrap paper. There is nothing more disappointing than to find you have used your last piece of treasured paper on an envelope that doesn't fit. If you open out an old envelope you will see that the basis is just a square or

You will find envelope-making much easier if you work on a cutting mat with a surface grid which helps greatly when measuring, ruling lines and making folds.

Self-healing cutting mat with surface grid

To make an envelope template:

STEP 1 Lay your card in the centre of a piece of scrap paper and rule around it, allowing a few millimetres all around for ease.

STEP 2 Using this ruled shape as a basis, calculate and rule the dimensions of the four triangular flaps, remembering that they should just overlap at the centre.

STEP 3 Lightly score the fold lines and cut out your template.

STEP 4 Check that the template fits your card and that the four flaps overlap nicely.

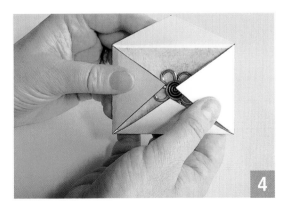

STEP 5 Use the template to draw out your actual envelope keeping all lines, angles and fold lines accurate by also referring to the grid on the cutting mat. Again, lightly score the fold lines before cutting out your envelope.

When cutting out, you can use a craft knife or scissors for a straight cut, or decorative scissors for a fancy edge, according to the style you want. Alternatively, you could tear or perforate the edge.

Practical Hint: keep all your templates for future use.

Ready-made envelope On those occasions when lots of envelopes are needed, e.g. for invitations or change of address, ready-made envelopes are ideal. These are available in lots of different colours and sizes, and you can decorate them with seals, stickers, stencilling, decorative scissors or paper punches.

Ready-made envelopes can be customized

CHAPTER FOUR

INTRODUCTION TO PROJECTS

The mini cards, gift tags and invitations in this section were created using the equipment, materials and techniques demonstrated in previous chapters. Each design is described in words and pictures which show you everything you need to know, and templates for any of the motifs can be traced directly from the line drawings. You may want to dive straight in and create your own design right now, but do have a quick look at the projects first; they are easily adaptable and you can change a greeting to your own special message, and introduce your own colour schemes, papers and accessories.

CONTEMPORARY LOOK

Simplicity is the key to a stylish, contemporary look. The basis of these three designs is a fold of bright, matt white watercolour paper which provides a beautiful contrast to touches of colour and metal. Minimal use of colour creates opportunity: if adding an envelope you could emphasise the contemporary feel with pure white, add colour, or maximise the metallic element.

LEAF

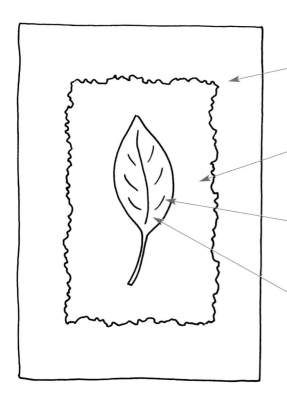

base:
fold of Frisk 320gsm
white watercolour paper

waste tissue from gold leafing
process, edge trimmed with
decorative scissors and attached
with glue stick

leaf drawn with medium-point stylus
on scrap of watercolour paper,
foiled, cut out, attached with PVA

matt gold leaf and bright gold
rub-down foil

This leaf motif was drawn –
using an embossing stylus –
into the soft surface of a scrap
of thick watercolour paper,
decorated with matt gold leaf
and bright gold rub-down foil,
then cut out. A sheet of waste
tissue from the gold leafing
process was trimmed with
decorative scissors to provide
the background for the leaf.

Refer to:
Embossed Effect (16)
Cutting Motifs (16)
Metal Leaf and Rub-down Foil
(26)
Folding Paper and Card (13)

DAISY

base:
fold of frisk 320gsm
white watercolour paper

scrap of bright pink painted
paper with torn edge,
attached with glue stick

matt gold leaf

daisy drawn with medium-
point stylus on scrap of
watercolour paper, foiled, cut
out, attached with PVA

A simple daisy motif was made
using the same method as the
leaf (see above), but here a torn
scrap of pink painted paper
provides a bright contrast.

Refer to:
Embossed Effect (16)
Cutting Motifs (16)
Tearing Paper (22)
Metal Leaf and Rub-down Foil
(26)
Folding Paper and Card (13)

HEART

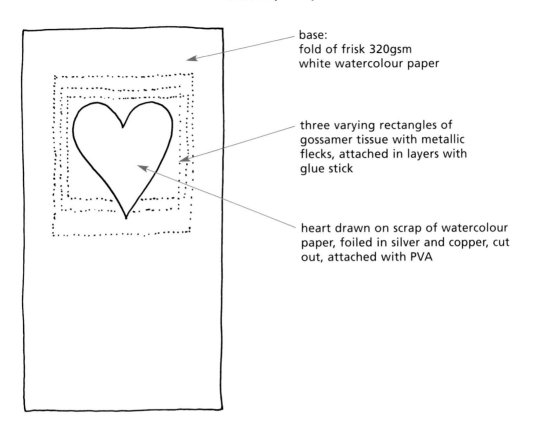

base:
fold of frisk 320gsm
white watercolour paper

three varying rectangles of
gossamer tissue with metallic
flecks, attached in layers with
glue stick

heart drawn on scrap of watercolour
paper, foiled in silver and copper, cut
out, attached with PVA

Layers of gossamer tissue, with gold
and silver particles, provide a
background patch for this heart motif
which is fashioned from thick, smooth
watercolour paper and covered in rub-
down silver and copper foils. Here, I
have used the design as a gift tag,
wrapping the gift in the same
gossamer tissue. The parcel is tied
with iridescent cellophane, entwined
with silver and copper embroidery
threads and the tag attached with a
tiny silver peg.

Refer to:
Cutting Motifs (16)
Metal Leaf and Rub-down Foil (26)
Folding Paper and Card (13)

SAY IT WITH FLOWERS

What better way to send your regards to someone than to say it with flowers? The designs here can be adapted for use as gift tags, thank you notes or mini greetings cards for almost any occasion. When used as gift tags you can add strings and beads, while for mini cards you could add a small message patch or tag – the possibilities are endless. Don't forget, you can also select your own colours and papers.

Simple but effective backgrounds for your flowers can be created by incorporating coloured paper, handmade paper, and torn or decorative edges. The flowers themselves are made with paper shapes, either cut out with small, sharp scissors or with decorative paper punches. Instructions for making all the flowers are given in the Decorative Techniques section (pages 28–33).

FLOWERS IN VASE

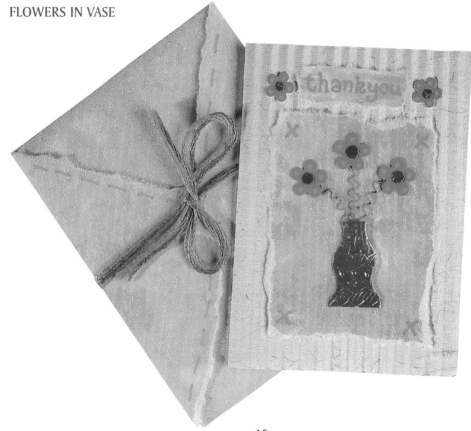

tiny circles of silver foiled paper, attached with PVA

scraps of orange gift wrap with torn edges, attached with glue stick

flower shapes punched from scrap of bright pink painted paper and attached with PVA

base:
fold of medium-weight, honeycomb textured white pastel paper front laminated with crimped, handmade, cream flecked paper

green yarn-covered wire, passed through paper crimper

lilac gel pen used for 'stitches', writing and decorations to flowers

vase cut from thick silver card, decorated with medium-point stylus and attached with PVA

These fun flowers with wiggly stems are very easy to make. Here, I have placed three in a silver vase on a scrap of printed orange gift wrap, which in turn sits on a base of cream crimped recycled paper. I have co-ordinated this design throughout by use of colour, torn edges and pen 'stitching'.

Extra touches that you can incorporate into your designs are tiny motifs on the reverse and easy-to-make decorated envelopes.

POSY OF FLOWERS

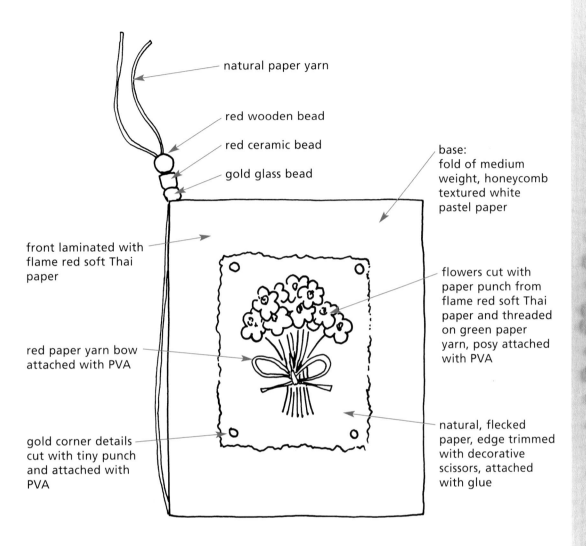

natural paper yarn

red wooden bead

red ceramic bead

gold glass bead

base:
fold of medium
weight, honeycomb
textured white
pastel paper

front laminated with
flame red soft Thai
paper

flowers cut with
paper punch from
flame red soft Thai
paper and threaded
on green paper
yarn, posy attached
with PVA

red paper yarn bow
attached with PVA

gold corner details
cut with tiny punch
and attached with
PVA

natural, flecked
paper, edge trimmed
with decorative
scissors, attached
with glue

This miniature posy of straight-stem
flowers with flame red paper petals
contrasts attractively with the simple
background in terms of both colour
and style, while the beads make it just
that little bit different.

Refer to:
Straight stem flower (29)
Laminating Paper (19)
Gluing Small Pieces (15))
Bows (20)
Decorative Paper Punches (23)
Folding Paper and Card (13)

PINK PANSY WITH BEAD CENTRE

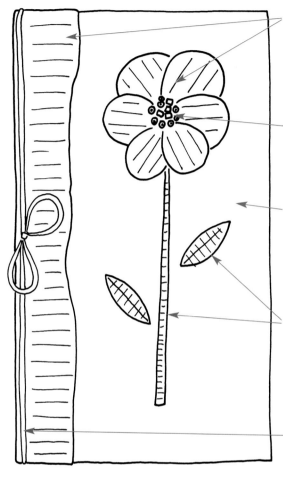

side trim and flower petals: lightweight watercolour paper with pale pink watercolour wash and crimped, all attached with PVA

lilac glass beads attached with PVA

base:
fold of medium weight, textured white watercolour paper

silver foiled paper, detailed on reverse with medium-point stylus and attached with glue stick

lilac 6 strand embroidery thread

A paper crimper will help you work wonders with just a small piece of coloured paper and, if you add a few beads and a silver stem, you have a pretty flower.

 Style Hint: make the top of the stem a fraction narrower than the base.

Refer to:	Paper Crimper (24)
Crimped flower (30)	Tearing Paper (22)
Collage (22)	Folding Paper and Card (13)

HEART FLOWER COLLAGE

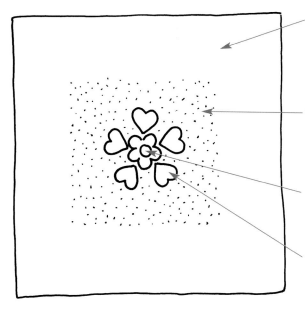

base:
flat square of Frisk 320gsm white watercolour paper

flat brushed square of pale green acrylic paint

pink pearl 3D paint in centre of flower

shapes punched from painted papers in deep aqua and pale pink, attached with PVA

A collage of punched paper shapes forms this flower motif and the loosely brushed mint green background is echoed in the gift wrap, which is tied with pink organza ribbon.

Refer to:
Paper punch flower (32)
Gluing Small Pieces (15)
Collage (22)
Flat Brush Painting (11)
Decorative Paper Punches (23)
3D Paint (26)

ORANGE FLOWER

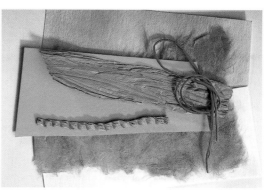

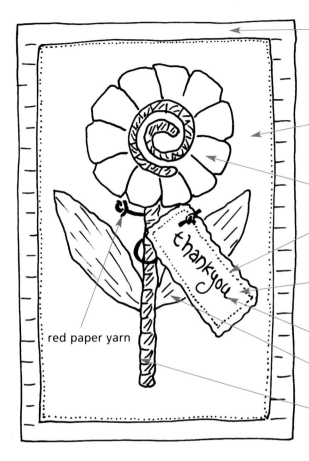

base:
fold of thick white watercolour paper, laminated on front with lightweight watercolour paper, which was first given a pale lilac watercolour wash, then crimped

panel of soft Thai paper in violet, straight cut edge decorated with punch wheel and attached with glue stick

orange, medium-weight, honeycomb textured pastel paper

scrap of orange paper with torn edge, threaded on red paper yarn

scrap of white paper with perforated and torn edge, attached with glue stick

green gel pen

green paper stripped from wire, attached with glue stick

green paper-covered wire, passed through paper crimper (also used for spiral flower centre)

red paper yarn

This single flower is a collage of papers and paper-covered wire and, luckily, I was able to find a small ready-made envelope which was an almost exact colour match.

A bold design such as this would translate well into any colour scheme, from bright metallic to natural and, of course, you can add your own message to the little label.

Refer to:
Curved petal flower with crimped stem (30)
Adding Your Message (14)
Spirals (21
Collage (22)
Paper Crimper (24)
Punch Wheel (24)
Folding Paper and Card (13)

Get Well Soon

GOLD FLOWER IN POT

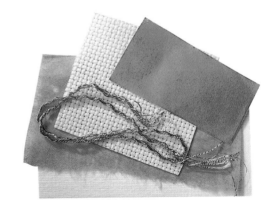

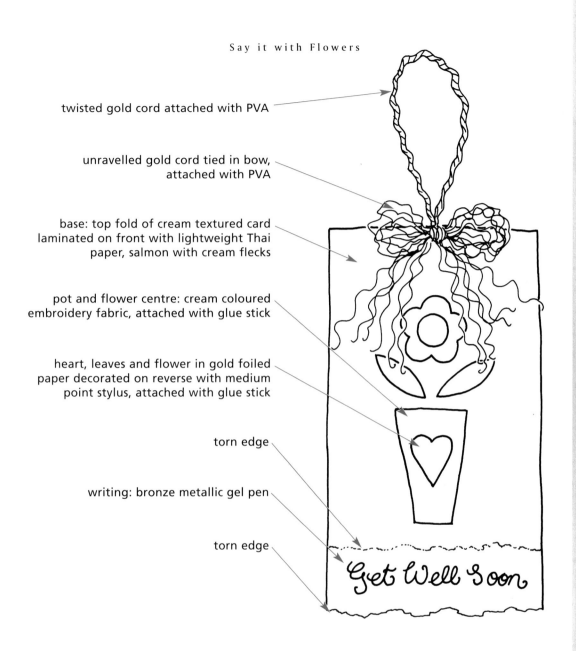

twisted gold cord attached with PVA

unravelled gold cord tied in bow, attached with PVA

base: top fold of cream textured card laminated on front with lightweight Thai paper, salmon with cream flecks

pot and flower centre: cream coloured embroidery fabric, attached with glue stick

heart, leaves and flower in gold foiled paper decorated on reverse with medium point stylus, attached with glue stick

torn edge

writing: bronze metallic gel pen

torn edge

Get Well Soon

Here, the matt, textural feel of fabric and delicate paper contrasts well with gleaming gold, while the cleanly cut elements of flower and pot contrast with torn edges and unravelled thread.

Refer to:
Paper and fabric collage flower (31)
Collage (22)
Tearing Paper (22)
Laminating Paper (19)
Folding Paper and Card (13)

HIPPIE STYLE

Handmade papers – available in stunning colours and textures to suit every kind of motif – make a superb starting point for gift tags and mini notelets. Add beads, a kitsch heart or flower, and you have super hippie styling. These couldn't be more effective, or more enjoyable to make.

The basis for these designs is a rectangle of handmade paper and a rectangle of lightweight paper, folded together (make them slightly larger than needed, so you can trim or tear them neatly to size).

Stitch along the fold: I used paper yarn, but you could choose anything from fine raffia to embroidery thread. Don't try to disguise the ends of the thread –

make a design feature by adding a knot or beads. The stunning colours and textures available in these decorative papers suit every kind of motif.

HIPPIE FLOWER

58

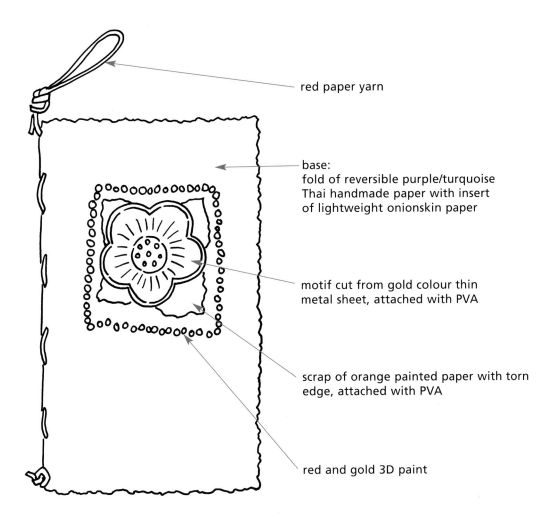

red paper yarn

base:
fold of reversible purple/turquoise
Thai handmade paper with insert
of lightweight onionskin paper

motif cut from gold colour thin
metal sheet, attached with PVA

scrap of orange painted paper with torn
edge, attached with PVA

red and gold 3D paint

Reversible purple/turquoise Thai handmade paper with an insert of lightweight onionskin paper is used here, and sewn together with fine red paper yarn. A torn patch of orange paper and metal flower motif are bordered in red and gold bead paint.

Refer to:
Sewing Paper (19)
Tearing Paper (22)
Thin Metal Sheet (27)
3D Paint (26)
Inserts (14
Folding Paper and Card (13)

HIPPIE HEART

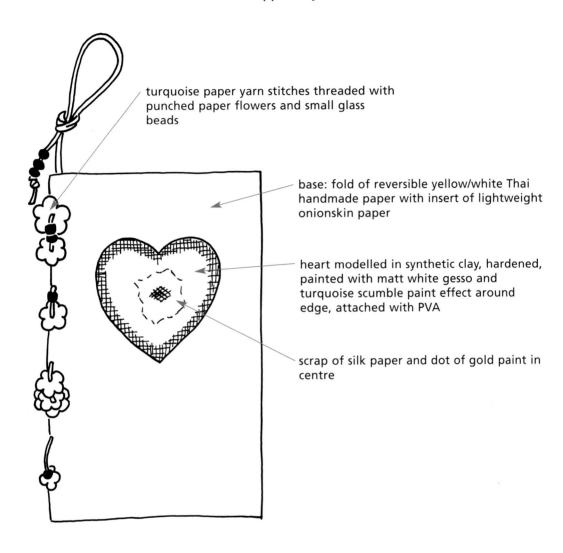

turquoise paper yarn stitches threaded with punched paper flowers and small glass beads

base: fold of reversible yellow/white Thai handmade paper with insert of lightweight onionskin paper

heart modelled in synthetic clay, hardened, painted with matt white gesso and turquoise scumble paint effect around edge, attached with PVA

scrap of silk paper and dot of gold paint in centre

Here, I have used reversible yellow/white Thai handmade paper as the background for a colourful heart motif which was modelled in synthetic clay, hardened, then decorated. Equally, you could make the heart in fabric, metal or thick paper. Punched flower shapes and beads were added while stitching the fold.

Refer to:
Sewing Paper (19)
Scumble (11)
Synthetic Modelling Clay (24)
Decorative Paper Punches (23)
Inserts (14)
Folding Paper and Card (13)

COPPER FLOWER

base:
fold of Mexican handmade bark paper with
insert of Chinese writing paper (a lightweight
cream laid paper), perforated and torn edges
to both

copper-effect flower attached with PVA

Refer to:
Inserts (14)
Punch Wheel (24)
Folding Paper and Card (13)
Decorative Envelopes (34–5)
Metal Leaf and Rub-down Foil (26)

Mexican handmade bark paper makes a
perfect background for this copper-
effect flower purchased from a bead
stall. I liked the simplicity of this
beautiful paper so I didn't add stitching,
but instead glued a panel of Chinese
writing paper inside. A small envelope
with perforated edges and copper-
foiled seal completes the design and
tones with this Thai silk gift wrap.

THAI CREAM

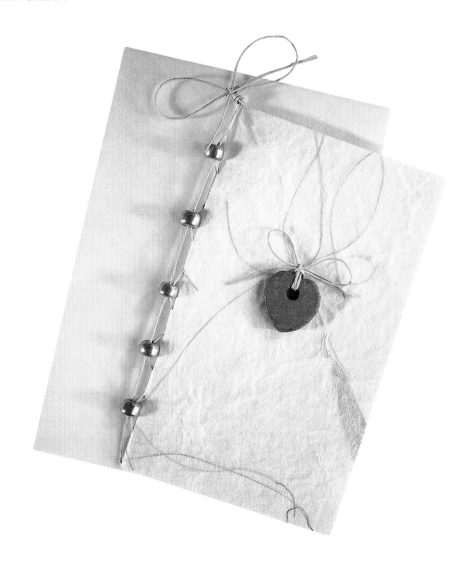

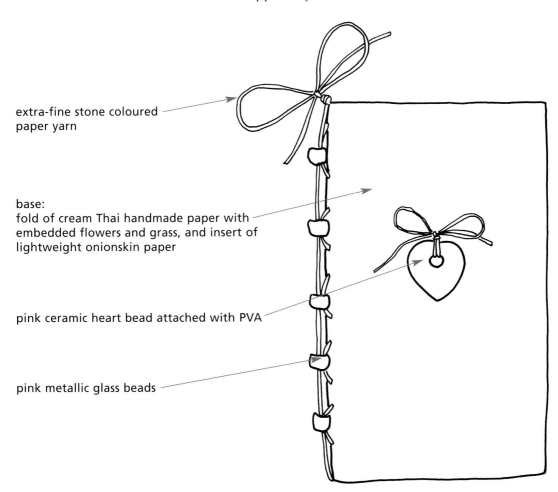

extra-fine stone coloured
paper yarn

base:
fold of cream Thai handmade paper with
embedded flowers and grass, and insert of
lightweight onionskin paper

pink ceramic heart bead attached with PVA

pink metallic glass beads

The subtle faded reds and browns of
bougainvillea flowers and grass fibres
embedded in this cream Thai handmade
paper suggested the colours for the
paper yarn and bead decorations. To
balance the elaborate beading, I have
teamed this design with a simple cream
envelope.

Refer to:
Sewing Paper (19)
Inserts (14)
Folding Paper and Card (13)

BABY LOVE

These designs are adaptable in terms of colour and motif. Traditional colours such as blue, pink and lemon always look sweet, while a white and silver combination is ideal for christenings; but you could ring the changes with peach, aqua or lilac. I have used a heart motif, teddy bear, pram, and bootees, but I am sure you can dream up many more!

PINK GINGHAM HEART

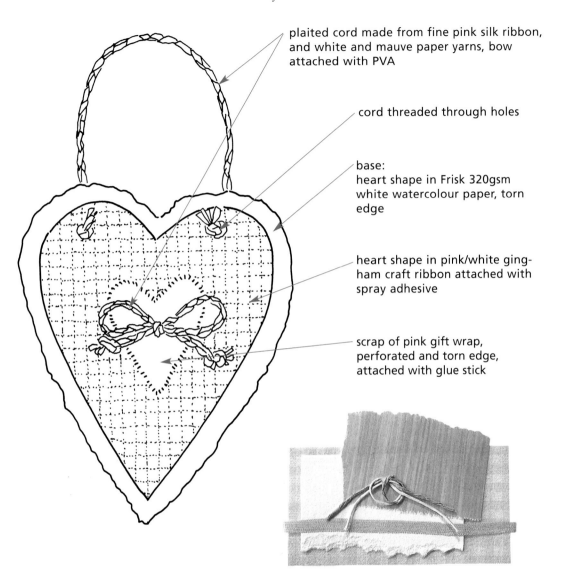

plaited cord made from fine pink silk ribbon, and white and mauve paper yarns, bow attached with PVA

cord threaded through holes

base:
heart shape in Frisk 320gsm white watercolour paper, torn edge

heart shape in pink/white gingham craft ribbon attached with spray adhesive

scrap of pink gift wrap, perforated and torn edge, attached with glue stick

This pink gingham heart is cut from cotton craft ribbon which is coated with a fabric stiffener during manufacture and so resists fraying. To add to the country feel, a plaited cord and bow were added and the background was given a torn edge, but a perforated or decorative cut edge could also be used.

Refer to:
Tearing Paper (22)
Bows (20)
Plaits (20)
Punch Wheel (24)
Sewing Paper (making holes in paper) (19)

BLUE GINGHAM HEART WITH TEDDY BEAR

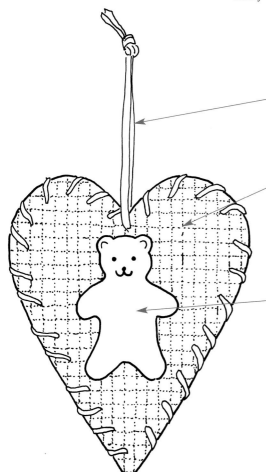

yellow paper yarn

base:
heart shape in white card covered with
blue/white gingham craft ribbon

teddy bear modelled in synthetic clay,
hardened, gesso undercoat, orange
watercolour wash and acrylic painted fea-
tures, attached with PVA

This blue gingham heart is also cut
from stiffened craft ribbon which was
bonded to white card with spray
adhesive. Yellow paper yarn stitches are
complemented by a tiny yellow teddy
bear modelled in synthetic clay,
hardened, and painted with
watercolour and acrylic paints.

Refer to:
Sewing Paper (19)
Synthetic Modelling Clay (24)

YELLOW GINGHAM HEART WITH PRAM

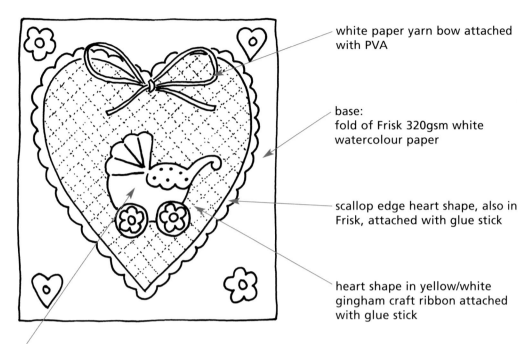

white paper yarn bow attached with PVA

base:
fold of Frisk 320gsm white watercolour paper

scallop edge heart shape, also in Frisk, attached with glue stick

heart shape in yellow/white gingham craft ribbon attached with glue stick

baby carriage, wheels, hearts and flowers drawn with medium-point embossing stylus on scrap of white watercolour paper, then cut out with small, sharp scissors and attached with PVA, yellow crayon highlights added

Fresh yellow gingham and tinted embossed effects have been used for this design. All the details on this card were drawn into thick, smooth watercolour paper using an embossing stylus, then cut out and glued in position, with a final touch of yellow crayon to emphasise the decorative details.

Refer to:
Embossed Effect (16)
Cutting Motifs (16
Bows (20)
Gluing Small Pieces (15)
Folding Paper and Card (13)

WHITE BOOTEES

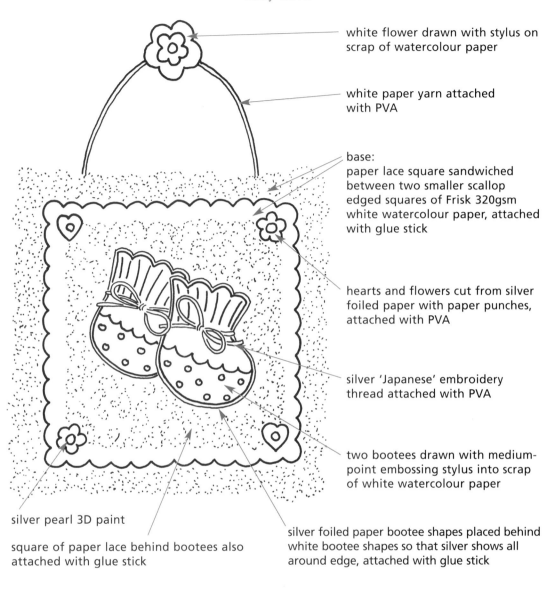

white flower drawn with stylus on scrap of watercolour paper

white paper yarn attached with PVA

base:
paper lace square sandwiched between two smaller scallop edged squares of Frisk 320gsm white watercolour paper, attached with glue stick

hearts and flowers cut from silver foiled paper with paper punches, attached with PVA

silver 'Japanese' embroidery thread attached with PVA

two bootees drawn with medium-point embossing stylus into scrap of white watercolour paper

silver pearl 3D paint

square of paper lace behind bootees also attached with glue stick

silver foiled paper bootee shapes placed behind white bootee shapes so that silver shows all around edge, attached with glue stick

Traditional white and silver have been used for this design, though you could replace the silver element with a pastel colour and change the look completely. A paper lace border emphasises the precious theme which is continued in the gift wrap of white Thai silk paper tied with silver gimp.

Refer to:
Embossed Effect (16)
Decorative Paper Punches (23)
3D Paint (26)
Decorative Scissors (23)
Gluing Small Pieces (15)

SAME BUT DIFFERENT!

These designs show how a few changes in colour and scale can make the same basic idea look completely different. The lilac and white colour scheme is elegant, whereas the fluorescent yellow, red and green design has a fun feel. When wrapping a small gift, you can take elements from any design and make a miniature gift tag, as demonstrated on this tiny package.

LILAC ELEGANCE

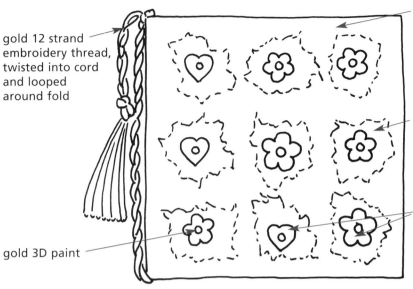

gold 12 strand embroidery thread, twisted into cord and looped around fold

base: fold of medium weight, textured white watercolour paper

torn scraps of lilac soft pulp paper with 'silk' threads, attached with PVA

gold 3D paint

punched heart and flower shapes cut from medium weight pastel paper and attached with PVA

Smudgy patches of torn lilac pulp paper make a great contrast for these crisply cut hearts and flowers. Further contrast is added with beads of gold pearl 3D paint and a sparkling gold cord. The mini-parcel and tiny tag are made with the same materials.

Refer to:
Decorative Paper Punches (23)
3D Paints (26)
Gluing Small Pieces (15)
Cords (20)
Folding Paper and Card (13)

FLUORESCENT FUN

torn scraps of red soft pulp paper with 'silk' threads, attached with PVA

base:
square of heavyweight watercolour paper, with torn edge, painted with fluorescent yellow gouache paint

lilac pearl 3D paint

punched flower shapes cut from green washed lightweight watercolour paper, and attached with PVA

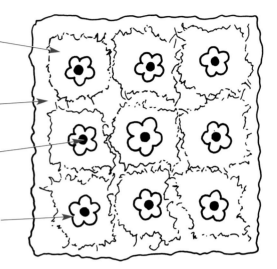

The torn outer edge of this brightly coloured tag emphasises the fun, handmade look. I have continued the bright colours in the gift wrap which, like the tiny torn pieces, is recycled pulp paper. This is decorated with punched flower shapes, and tied with fine yellow ricrac braid. A final touch is the tiny green wooden peg attaching the gift tag.

Refer to:
Tearing Paper (22)
Decorative Paper Punches (23)
3D Paint (26)
Gluing Small Pieces (15)

YOU'RE INVITED TO A PARTY!

Planning a party? Why not let the fun start here by making your own special invitations? If you want to make lots of cards, a speedy and effective method is to use cut shapes or draw simple motifs in 3D paint.

Party details can be word-processed or photocopied and added as a folded leaf inside, or be rubber-stamped directly inside the card. Word processors and photocopiers have their limitations regarding the sort of paper you can use, whereas stamping can be applied to almost any sort of paper.

CUP CAKE

pompom attached with PVA

base:
fold of textured, medium weight, white watercolour paper

bright pink painted paper, decorated with yellow gel pen and attached with glue stick

lilac gel pen 'stitching'

yellow paper with glitterglaze finish, crimped, attached with glue stick

punched flower and heart shapes cut from bright pink painted paper and decorated with yellow gel pen

Tempting collage cup cakes are great fun for children to make and you can continue the food theme by wrapping these invitations in paper lace doilies.

Refer to:
Adding Your Message (14)
Gluing Small Pieces (15)
Collage (22)
Decorative Paper Punches (23)
Gluing Pompoms (15)
Pen 'Stitching' (19)
Paper Crimper (24)
Glitterglaze (24)
Folding Paper and Card (13)

CHAMPAGNE CELEBRATION

base:
fold of Frisk 320gsm white
watercolour paper

sparkling silver 3D paint

flat brushed panel in mint green
acrylic paint

This champagne glass motif has quite a contemporary feel. It is quick to make and you could add numbers for a special celebration – say an 18th or 21st birthday. I have added a tiny sparkling star to the flap of the matt silver ready-made envelope.

 Style Hint: try teaming sparkling and matt elements in the same colour.

Refer to:
Adding Your Message (14)
3D Paint (26)
Flat Brush Painting (11)
Folding Paper and Card (13)

BIRTHDAY CAKE

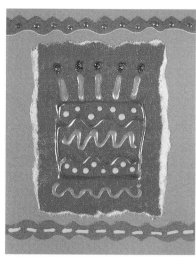

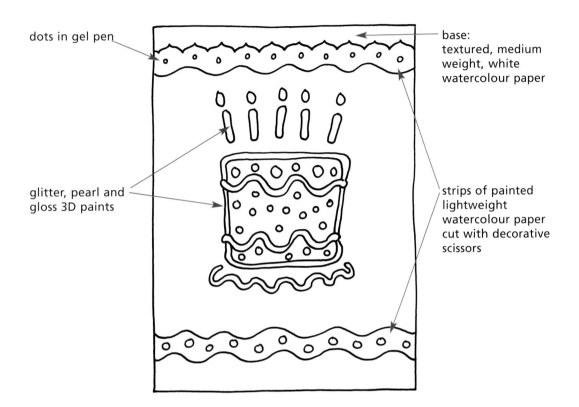

dots in gel pen

base: textured, medium weight, white watercolour paper

glitter, pearl and gloss 3D paints

strips of painted lightweight watercolour paper cut with decorative scissors

As we have discovered, a simple colour change can give any design a different look. This birthday cake is very adaptable in terms of colour schemes and decorations. I have teamed this design with a ready-made envelope sealed with a smiley-face sticker. If you are unsure about painting the cakes straight onto cards you could paint them on scraps of paper, then add them as torn motifs, as I did with the pink and orange version.

Refer to:
Adding Your Message (14
3D Paint (26)

Decorative Scissors (23)
Tearing Paper (22)
Folding Paper and Card (13)

HAPPY DOG

party hat cut from painted paper and decorated with sparkly 3D paint

base:
dog shape cut from Frisk 320gsm white watercolour paper

eyes and nose, black fibre tip pen

collar, green crayon

toes, pink crayon

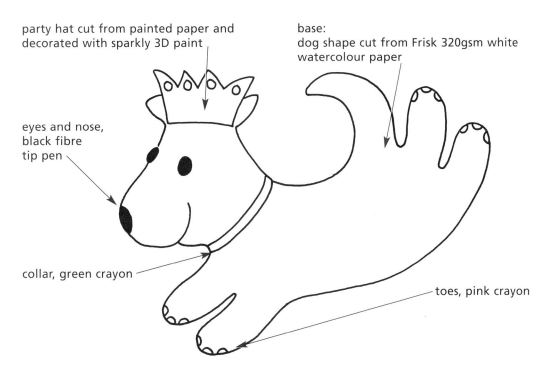

Happy Dog was drawn on thick white watercolour paper, using a medium-point stylus, then the image cut out and details added with pen and crayon.

The party hat, made from coloured paper, was trimmed with 3D sparkly paint. Party details were rubber-stamped on a square of very lightweight paper, which was then folded and tucked into Happy Dog's mouth.

Size C7 envelopes fit the Happy Dog design exactly and these transparent ones add extra fun.

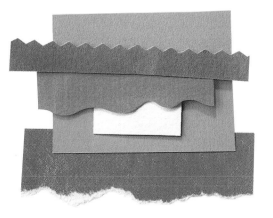

Refer to:
Embossed Effect (16)
Cutting Motifs (16)
3D Paint (26)
Adding Your Message (14)
Stencilling (12)

COSY CAT

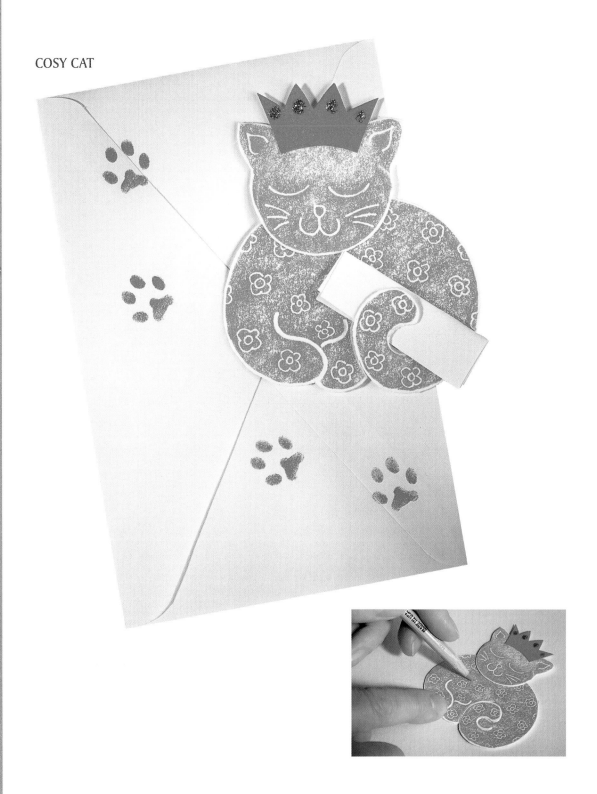

party hat cut from painted paper and decorated with sparkly 3D paint

base:
cat shape cut from Frisk 320gsm white watercolour paper

coloured and highlighted with mauve and pink crayon

A medium-point stylus was used to draw Cosy Cat on thick white watercolour paper; the image was then cut out and decorated with the stylus and crayon.

The party hat, made from coloured paper, was embellished with 3D sparkly paint. Party details were rubber stamped on a square of very lightweight paper, which was then folded and tucked into Cosy Cat's tail.

As a final touch, the envelope was decorated with a paw-print stencil.

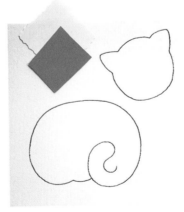

Refer to:
Embossed Effect (16)
Cutting Motifs (16)
3D Paint (26)
Adding Your Message (14)
Stencilling (12)

DESIGNS FOR ANY OCCASION

You may have an occasion in mind which these designs will suit but you can also trim them up, pare them down, or use different colour schemes and materials: use just silver and white for the Kitsch Heart, substitute tiny silk flowers on Pompoms Galore, or find some different sugarcraft cutters to use on the Star background.

KITSCH HEART

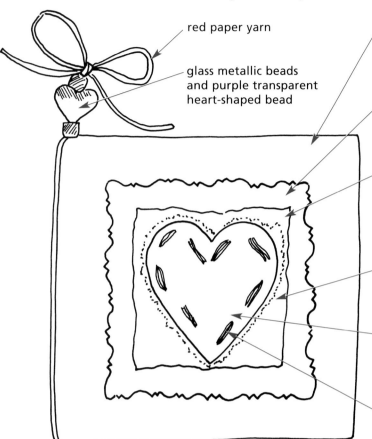

red paper yarn

glass metallic beads
and purple transparent
heart-shaped bead

base:
fold of white card, front
laminated with mauve pulp
paper with 'silk' fibres

pink painted paper with
decorative cut edge, attached
with glue stick

scrap of red honeycomb
textured paper decorated
with mixed metallic coloured
rub-down foil and attached
with glue stick

heart shape in mauve pulp
paper with torn edge,
attached with glue stick

heart shape: watercolour
paper decorated with red
wash and traces of gold leaf,
and attached with glue stick

stitches in silver 'Japanese'
embroidery thread

This kitsch design composed in red,
pink and mauve, with a touch of gold
and silver, makes a great mini card or,
as here, can be dressed up with cord
and beads to create a gift tag.

Style Hint: sometimes it's great
to go OTT and team red with
bright pink, gold with silver etc.

Refer to:	
Metal Leaf and Rub-down Foil (26)	Sewing Paper (19)
Laminating Paper (19)	Tearing Paper (22)
Decorative Scissors (23)	Folding Paper and Card (13)

STAR

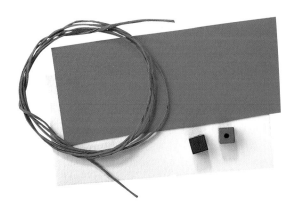

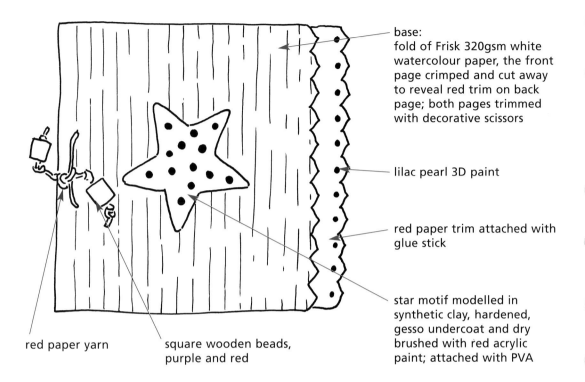

base:
fold of Frisk 320gsm white
watercolour paper, the front
page crimped and cut away
to reveal red trim on back
page; both pages trimmed
with decorative scissors

lilac pearl 3D paint

red paper trim attached with
glue stick

star motif modelled in
synthetic clay, hardened,
gesso undercoat and dry
brushed with red acrylic
paint; attached with PVA

red paper yarn

square wooden beads,
purple and red

Synthetic modelling clay was used to
make this star motif, which was
decorated (after hardening and cooling)
with dry brush strokes and lilac pearl
3D paint. Sugarcraft cutters are ideal
for making these small motifs.

Refer to:
Synthetic Modelling Clay (24)
Decorative Scissors (23)
3D Paint (26)
Paper Crimper (24)
Sewing Paper (for making holes in
paper) (19)
Folding Paper and Card (13)

POMPOMS GALORE!

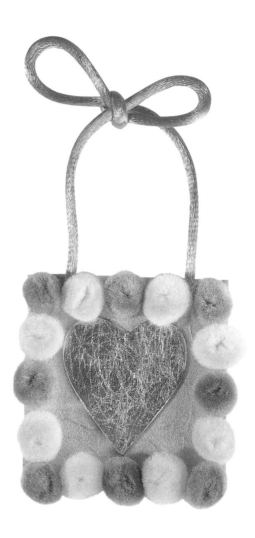

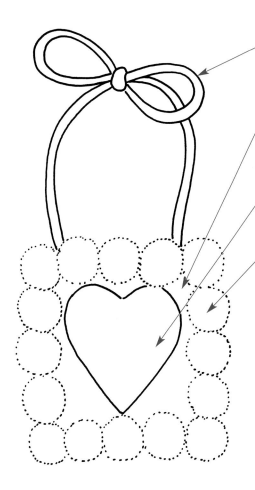

pink rattail braid attached with PVA

base:
small rectangle of white card, laminated with pink 'silk' paper attached with glue stick

heart shape covered with siver foil and attached with glue stick

mauve and pink pompoms attached with PVA

Surprise someone! These pink and mauve pompoms are teamed with a silver heart for a really fun gift tag. What colour to use for gift wrap? Pink, of course!

Refer to:
Gluing Pompoms (15)
Bows (20)
Foil Covered Motifs (17)
Laminating Paper (19)

SAILING BOAT

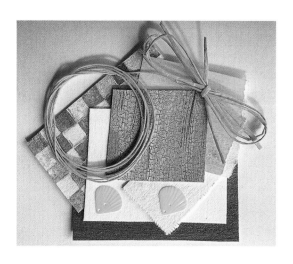

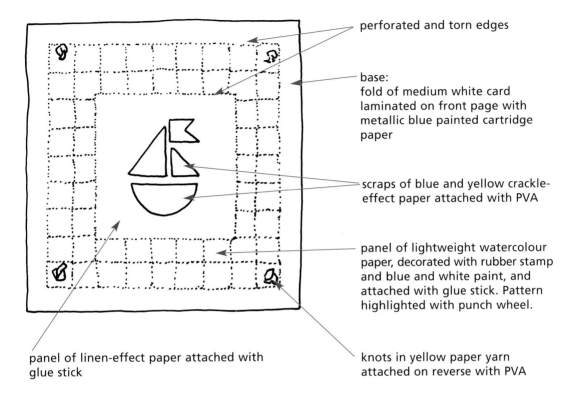

perforated and torn edges

base:
fold of medium white card
laminated on front page with
metallic blue painted cartridge
paper

scraps of blue and yellow crackle-
effect paper attached with PVA

panel of lightweight watercolour
paper, decorated with rubber stamp
and blue and white paint, and
attached with glue stick. Pattern
highlighted with punch wheel.

panel of linen-effect paper attached with
glue stick

knots in yellow paper yarn
attached on reverse with PVA

The techniques of stamping,
perforating, and collage are combined
to create this little sailing boat design,
complete with decorative knots. I
found some shell-style sequins to trim
the matching envelope.

Refer to:
Crackle Finish (11)
Collage (22)
Printing (12)
Punch Wheel (24)
Decorative Knots and Stitches (20)
Folding Paper and Card (13)
Decorative Envelopes (34–5)

STARFISH

turquoise and gold glass beads

stone-coloured paper yarn

base:
fold of medium-weight, honeycomb textured pastel paper with torn edges

panel of lightweight watercolour paper, painted with metallic blue, and attached with glue stick

wavy edge cut with decorative scissors and sewn with stone coloured paper yarn

starfish motif, cut from gold-coloured thin metal sheet and attached with PVA

The nautical theme is continued with this gold metal starfish on a blue metallic paper patch with stitching and beaded trim. I have used the same blue metallic paint, thinned and applied with a bristle brush, to produce a toning gift wrap.

Refer to:
Thin Metal Sheet (27)
Sewing Paper (19)
Folding Paper and Card (13)

HOT AIR BALLOON

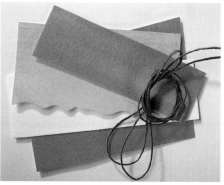

turquoise paper yarn

base:
luggage tag shape cut in Frisk 320gsm
white watercolour paper, using wavy edge
decorative scissors

flat brushed pale blue acrylic paint

hot air balloon created with decorative
strips of coloured paper

turquoise paper yarn

punched shapes cut from painted paper

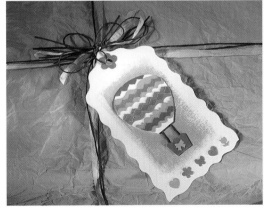

This luggage-style tag with hot air balloon motif is ideal decoration for a leaving gift. The loosely brushed blue sky background and wavy edge add a sense of movement, while crushed tissue paper and paper yarn make a simple and inexpensive gift wrap.

Refer to:
Decorative Paper Punches (23)
Decorative Scissors (23)
Gluing Small Pieces (15)

99

WEDDING

These wedding gift tags could be developed as cards, or even as place cards or invitations. I have used traditional colour schemes of white with silver, and cream with gold, but touches of colour could be introduced, especially if you have engagements or anniversaries in mind.

WHITE LACE

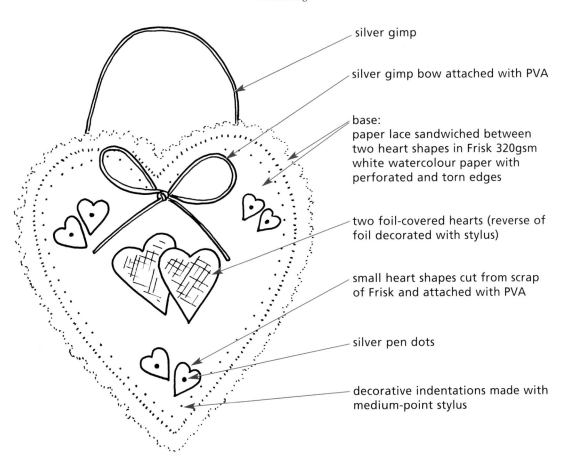

silver gimp

silver gimp bow attached with PVA

base:
paper lace sandwiched between
two heart shapes in Frisk 320gsm
white watercolour paper with
perforated and torn edges

two foil-covered hearts (reverse of
foil decorated with stylus)

small heart shapes cut from scrap
of Frisk and attached with PVA

silver pen dots

decorative indentations made with
medium-point stylus

A border of delicate lace paper is
sandwiched between two matt white
paper hearts and the front is decorated
using embossing and foiling techniques.
This gift tag could add an individual
touch to a store-bought gift wrap.

Refer to:
Gluing Small Pieces (15)
Foil Covered Motifs (17)
Bows (20)
Cutting Motifs (16)
Punch Wheel (24)

CREAM AND GOLD

heart shape covered in soft textured ivory paper and attached with PVA

base:
fold of medium-weight, textured cream watercolour paper, with insert of white lightweight paper; front pages cut to reveal inside of back page which has gold leafing to the edge

fine bamboo paper yarn, tied in bow and wrapped around hearts, and attached with PVA

heart shape drawn on scrap of Frisk with medium-point stylus, decorated with matt gold leaf, then attached with PVA

This fold of textured papers and gold effects is trimmed back to enhance the layered look. As a gift tag, this design could be teamed with a simple ready-made envelope in gold, cream or chamois, which would complement the papyrus gift wrap, tied with a loose twist of flat paper yarn and gold embroidery thread. If you are using a simpler gift wrap, or making a mini greetings card, you could create a decorative envelope such as the papyrus folded wrap shown on the right.

Refer to:
Paper-covered Shapes (18)
Embossed Effect (16)
Bows (20)
Metal Leaf and Rub-down Foil (26)
Decorative Scissors (23)
Inserts (14)
Folding Paper and Card (13)

NEW HOME AND
CHANGE OF ADDRESS

Whether wishing someone good luck in their new home or advertising your own change of address, these designs will adapt readily.

Change of address cards need to be made in multiples which can be assembled quite speedily, so I have used torn shapes, cut shapes and decorative paper punches. Details of your address can be produced on a word processor or photocopier and added as an insert. Alternatively, you could obtain a custom-made stamp with all your details. Stamps, readily available by mail order, are quite inexpensive and can be made to your own design.

COTTAGE ON A
GREEN LAWN

text created on word processor, edges of paper torn, and attached with glue stick

base:
fold of medium-weight, yellow, honeycomb pastel paper

punched flower shapes decorated with lilac gel pen and attached with PVA

panel of green gift wrap paper with torn edge, attached with glue stick

house created from scraps of paper and punched shapes, roof crimped

leaves and stems drawn with green gel pen

This cottage on a green lawn is made from torn shapes, cut shapes and paper punch motifs. For added interest, the roof is made in lightly speckled, crimped paper and the flowers have been detailed with bright gel pen. The ready-made envelope was quickly decorated with a paper punch.

Refer to:
Tearing Paper (22)
Decorative Paper Punches (23)
Gluing Small Pieces (15)
Adding Your Message (14)
Collage (22)
Paper Crimper (24)
Inserts (14)
Folding Paper and Card (13)

ANOTHER COTTAGE!

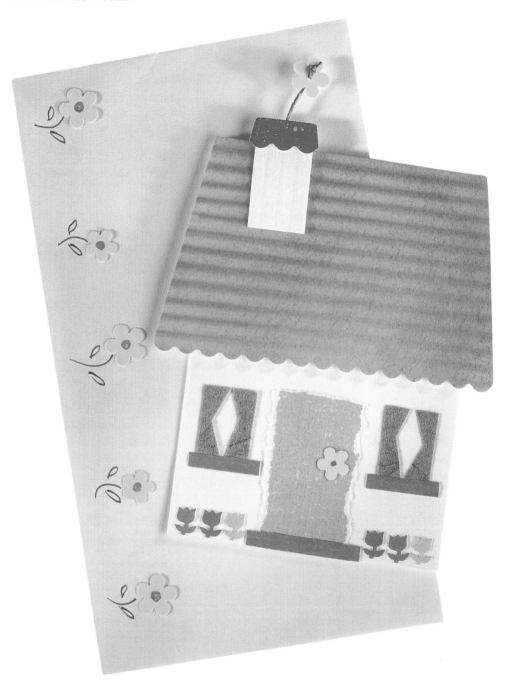

green paper yarn

scrap of painted red paper with fine yellow splatter, attached with glue stick

cartridge paper, tan washed and crimped, edges cut with scallop scissors; attached with glue stick

scrap of white crimped Frisk attached with PVA

base:
fold of Frisk 320gsm white watercolour paper

mauve soft pulp 'silk' paper, attached with glue stick

green painted medium-weight paper, attached with glue stick

pale blue crackle effect with torn edge and attached with glue stick

punched flower shapes in various colours and attached with PVA

bronze gel pen centre

Cottages are such fun to make that I couldn't resist another one! Again I have used crimped paper, cut motifs and paper punches, but the roof lifts up on this one, to reveal your message (see picture on page 14). Inexpensive white envelopes can be decorated with punched paper shapes and pen.

Refer to:	
Paper Crimper (24)	Splatter (10)
Decorative Paper Punches (23)	Adding Your Message (14)
Collage (22)	Gluing Small Pieces (15)
Crackle Finish (11)	Tearing Paper (22)
	Folding Paper and Card (13)

MATERIALS USED

I obtain my art and craft materials from many sources and am continually discovering new products but, on this occasion, I would particularly like to thank the following:

Artoz Limited, creative paper and stationery products, for C7 envelopes, widely available in stationery, art, card and gift shops throughout the UK. Artoz products are also available at the London Graphic Centre: mail order on 020 7240 0095 or visit the London Graphic Centre's web site at www.londongraphics.co.uk and go to 'retail' then 'covent garden' for an on-line catalogue.

Fiskars UK Limited, art and craft equipment, for paper crimper. For details of products and stockists in UK telephone 01656 655595. Available worldwide.

Inscribe Limited, art and craft materials, for gesso, liquid acrylic paints, glitter glaze, crackle finish, Tulip 3D paints and decorative scissors. Widely available throughout UK. For details of products and stockists, telephone 01420 475747.

Paperdeluxe, suppliers of spun paper yarns and decorative papercraft packs, 17 High Street, Great Houghton, Barnsley, South Yorkshire S72 0AA. E-mail: paperdeluxe@hotmail.com

S for Stamps, stamps and accessories. Shop and mail order, 15 Southcroft Road, Rutherglen, Glasgow, Scotland G73 1SP, telephone 0141 613 2680.

ABOUT THE AUTHOR

A member of an artistic family, Glennis Gilruth has drawn and painted throughout her life. After attending the University of Huddersfield as a mature student, gaining BA (Hons) in Surface Pattern, she now works as an illustrator and designer. Glennis finds her inspiration in people, places and animals and, whether travelling or at home in Yorkshire, these images, their colours and patterns, find their way into her designs.

INDEX

TITLES AVAILABLE FROM
GMC PUBLICATIONS

BOOKS

WOODCARVING

Beginning Woodcarving	GMC Publications
Carving Architectural Detail in Wood: The Classical Tradition	Frederick Wilbur
Carving Birds & Beasts	GMC Publications
Carving Classical Styles in Wood	Frederick Wilbur
Carving the Human Figure: Studies in Wood and Stone	Dick Onians
Carving Nature: Wildlife Studies in Wood	Frank Fox-Wilson
Celtic Carved Lovespoons: 30 Patterns	Sharon Littley & Clive Griffin
Decorative Woodcarving (New Edition)	Jeremy Williams
Elements of Woodcarving	Chris Pye
Figure Carving in Wood: Human and Animal Forms	Sara Wilkinson
Lettercarving in Wood: A Practical Course	Chris Pye
Relief Carving in Wood: A Practical Introduction	Chris Pye
Woodcarving for Beginners	GMC Publications
Woodcarving Made Easy	Cynthia Rogers
Woodcarving Tools, Materials & Equipment (New Edition in 2 vols.)	Chris Pye

WOODTURNING

Bowl Turning Techniques Masterclass	Tony Boase
Chris Child's Projects for Woodturners	Chris Child
Decorating Turned Wood: The Maker's Eye	Liz & Michael O'Donnell
Green Woodwork	Mike Abbott
A Guide to Work-Holding on the Lathe	Fred Holder
Keith Rowley's Woodturning Projects	Keith Rowley
Making Screw Threads in Wood	Fred Holder
Segmented Turning: A Complete Guide	Ron Hampton
Turned Boxes: 50 Designs	Chris Stott
Turning Green Wood	Michael O'Donnell
Turning Pens and Pencils	Kip Christensen & Rex Burningham
Wood for Woodturners	Mark Baker
Woodturning: Forms and Materials	John Hunnex
Woodturning: A Foundation Course (New Edition)	Keith Rowley
Woodturning: A Fresh Approach	Robert Chapman
Woodturning: An Individual Approach	Dave Regester
Woodturning: A Source Book of Shapes	John Hunnex
Woodturning Masterclass	Tony Boase
Woodturning Projects: A Workshop Guide to Shapes	Mark Baker

WOODWORKING

Beginning Picture Marquetry	Lawrence Threadgold
Carcass Furniture	GMC Publications
Celtic Carved Lovespoons: 30 Patterns	Sharon Littley & Clive Griffin
Celtic Woodcraft	Glenda Bennett
Celtic Woodworking Projects	Glenda Bennett
Complete Woodfinishing (Revised Edition)	Ian Hosker

David Charlesworth's Furniture-Making Techniques	David Charlesworth
David Charlesworth's Furniture-Making Techniques – Volume 2	David Charlesworth
Furniture Projects with the Router	Kevin Ley
Furniture Restoration (Practical Crafts)	Kevin Jan Bonner
Furniture Restoration: A Professional at Work	John Lloyd
Furniture Workshop	Kevin Ley
Green Woodwork	Mike Abbott
History of Furniture: Ancient to 1900	Michael Huntley
Intarsia: 30 Patterns for the Scrollsaw	John Everett
Making Heirloom Boxes	Peter Lloyd
Making Screw Threads in Wood	Fred Holder
Making Woodwork Aids and Devices	Robert Wearing
Mastering the Router	Ron Fox
Pine Furniture Projects for the Home	Dave Mackenzie
Router Magic: Jigs, Fixtures and Tricks to Unleash your Router's Full Potential	Bill Hylton
Router Projects for the Home	GMC Publications
Router Tips & Techniques	Robert Wearing
Routing: A Workshop Handbook	Anthony Bailey
Routing for Beginners (Revised and Expanded Edition)	Anthony Bailey
Stickmaking: A Complete Course	Andrew Jones & Clive George
Stickmaking Handbook	Andrew Jones & Clive George
Storage Projects for the Router	GMC Publications
Success with Sharpening	Ralph Laughton
Veneering: A Complete Course	Ian Hosker
Veneering Handbook	Ian Hosker
Wood: Identification & Use	Terry Porter
Woodworking Techniques and Projects	Anthony Bailey
Woodworking with the Router: Professional Router Techniques any Woodworker can Use	Bill Hylton & Fred Matlack

UPHOLSTERY

The Upholsterer's Pocket Reference Book	David James
Upholstery: A Complete Course (Revised Edition)	David James
Upholstery Restoration	David James
Upholstery Techniques & Projects	David James
Upholstery Tips and Hints	David James

DOLLS' HOUSES AND MINIATURES

1/12 Scale Character Figures for the Dolls' House	James Carrington
Americana in 1/12 Scale: 50 Authentic Projects	Joanne Ogreenc & Mary Lou Santovec
The Authentic Georgian Dolls' House	Brian Long
A Beginners' Guide to the Dolls' House Hobby	Jean Nisbett
Celtic, Medieval and Tudor Wall Hangings in 1/12 Scale Needlepoint	Sandra Whitehead
Creating Decorative Fabrics: Projects in 1/12 Scale	Janet Storey

CRAFTS

GARDENING

MAGAZINES

WOODTURNING
WOODCARVING
FURNITURE & CABINETMAKING
THE ROUTER
NEW WOODWORKING
THE DOLLS' HOUSE MAGAZINE
BLACK & WHITE PHOTOGRAPHY
OUTDOOR PHOTOGRAPHY
KNITTING
GUILD NEWS

The above represents a selection of the titles
currently published or scheduled to be published.
All are available direct from the Publishers
or through bookshops, newsagents and
specialist retailers.
To place an order, or to obtain a complete
catalogue, contact:

GMC PUBLICATIONS,
166 HIGH STREET, LEWES,
EAST SUSSEX BN7 1XU, UNITED KINGDOM
TEL: 01273 488005 FAX: 01273 478606

E-mail: pubs@thegmcgroup.com
Website: www.gmcbooks.com

Orders by credit card are accepted